Seasonings
prayers of praise and complaint

Seasonings

prayers of praise and complaint

Reverend Allen M. Comstock

illustrations by
Reverend Cara B. Hochhalter

foreword by Tinky Weisblat

Haley's

Athol, Massachusetts

Haley's
488 South Main Street
Athol, MA 01331
haley.antique@verizon.net • 978.249.9400

Cover illustration by Cara Hochhalter.

Copy edited by Eveline MacDougall.

Proof read by Debra Ellis.

International Standard Book Numbers
    trade paperback: 978-1-956055-05-4
    ebook: 978-1-956055-06-1

Library of Congress Cataloging-in-Publication Data pending

for the late

Hannah Landstrom Burrington

September 10, 1901-February 4, 1997

who encouraged the

creation of *Seasonings*

As I struggled to learn how to write sermons
while just winging it with pastoral prayers,
she said to me very solemnly,
"You know, the pastoral prayer is every bit as important
as the sermon, if not more so."
After that, I never wrote another sermon,
but I *always* wrote the pastoral prayers.

—Reverend Allen M. Comstock

As poems, these are pretty good prayers.

Contents

Advent

Christmas

Epiphany

Lent

Holy Week and Eastertide

Prayers Too Darn Beautiful
to be Stuffed in a Drawer

a foreword by Tinky Weisblat

I know both Allen Comstock (known to one and all as "Mick") and Cara Hochhalter. I am a member of the Federated Church in Charlemont, Massachusetts, where they served as minister at different times, Mick for eighteen years and Cara for ten. Mick performed the funeral service for my father; Cara, the service for my mother.

Mick's talent as a writer/poet and Cara's as an artist were on display when each of them inhabited the pulpit. Most of the words in this book were written for services Mick led. Cara frequently conveyed her feelings about the week's scripture lessons by including her art in the church bulletin.

In fact, I would like to claim full credit for this book's appearance in the world. Service after service, year after year, I told Mick that his prayers were too darn beautiful to be stuffed in a drawer and forgotten after each service. Of course, other people probably told him this, too. I have a loud voice, however, so I'm claiming credit.

Despite my long-time membership in the church where I met Mick and Cara, and despite my affection for each of them, I may not be the ideal person to write about their book of prayer poems or about any such book. I'm frankly not particularly religious. I go to church more for music and fellowship than for any words or visions from on high.

And yet … it may well be my lack of religious certainty that makes me the ideal reader for *Seasonings*. Against my will and my reason, Mick's words and Cara's drawings come close to making a believer of me. They situate God in the natural and human worlds in which we live.

The book follows the Christian church calendar, beginning in Advent and ending in the fall as Advent is about to return. It also follows the rhythm and the physical reality of the seasons we experience year after year, grounding faith in nature.

Yes, we read words about Mary and Joseph and Jesus and angels and see pictures of them. We also read about, and look at images of, birds and plants and snowstorms and autumn leaves. And Mick and Cara relate those images to the God in whom they trust.

To Mick, each season and its related seasonings offer more questions than answers. Each prayer is not just a request for divine intervention but is more importantly a reminder that we humans must seek out the qualities we associate with God: compassion, humility, justice, and especially love.

The complex rhythm of Mick's words and the soft charcoal lines of Cara's drawings complement each other and touch the reader with a blend of simplicity and depth. I freely admit that I was moved to tears several times while reading *Seasonings*. The book is simultaneously very human, a little funny, and gently profound. Perhaps, Mick and Cara are trying to tell us, those characteristics define God. I hope so.

I encourage readers to sift through the book a little at a time and to learn from it. I hope *Seasonings* will open hearts to its wisdom, to its questioning, to its humor, to its sweetness, and above all to all its faith that we can all be touched by what Lincoln called "the better angels of our nature."

Tinky Weisblat is a writer, historian, and singer who lives in Hawley, Massachusetts. She is the author of *The Pudding Hollow Cookbook*; *Pulling Taffy*; *Love, Laughter, and Rhubarb*; and *Pot Luck: Random Acts of Cooking*.

ADVENT

Our hearts are stirred.

Endings and Beginnings

Endings and beginnings come so close upon each other that we can scarcely tell one from the other, dear God. Dying and birth, sadness and mirth merge and mix with painful dissonance and sudden surprising harmonies.

We grieve for the passing of time, and knowing what we know now, we yearn backward to have the time to do over again and better.

Yet into this sad season you are born to bear time's weight, to breathe your life into the time to come, to fold our grieving into your own and transform our yearning into hoping. We can't yet see what we're hoping for. But our hearts are stirred, and they make motions of opening as they unfold reluctantly to give you thanks for your constant coming among us.

A Christmas Present

Dear God, the words with which we speak and sing this season betray our deepest yearnings. For whether we are young or whether we are old, we pray for a Christmas *present*—some sacred time and place saved, if only for a moment, from the inexorable march of our past into our future—some powerful and gentle new *now* that does not scatter and disperse but *gathers* and treasures and nurses every new infant instant.

There we are, caught out in our Christmas wishing, for we wish *ourselves* born in Bethlehem and you, dear Father, our Mother.

Are we to be caught, then, in a web of our own yearning's making and return from Bethlehem as bitter Herods wreaking havoc on the land, trying to kill what we saw born there because we found *you* and not just ourselves born in that lowly manger?

Or shall we finally allow our hearts to be made as wombs and consent to give *you* birth and so ourselves this year of years?

Kneel us next to the archangel waiting for Mary to answer.

Mary

Why is Gabriel, who was so puffed up and abristle with your importance and his own and with his impatience with Zechariah, almost shy, now, as he approaches Mary? It feels like all his history with you and with humankind has fallen away, does him no good at all—hasn't prepared him for this moment. Up until now in all human history, he has announced, pronounced, demanded, promised, or warned, but now he offers, now he asks, now he waits for an answer he doesn't already know.

Quiet the memories that would push us also through this moment and beyond, because we've already heard this story over and over again from beginning to end. Kneel us next to the archangel waiting for Mary to answer. Find in our hearts the hope for her that she will answer "No" and marry Joseph and bear their children and live a long life and die simply with the honor due any mother.

And maybe even find in us such wild courage as would say yes to the angel in her place and bear for her this child and all that she will have to bear for us.

And finally touch and rouse everything in us that needs her to say yes and is grateful that she did and would sing with Gabriel and with Elizabeth and with the centuries: *Hail, Mary, Mother of God!*

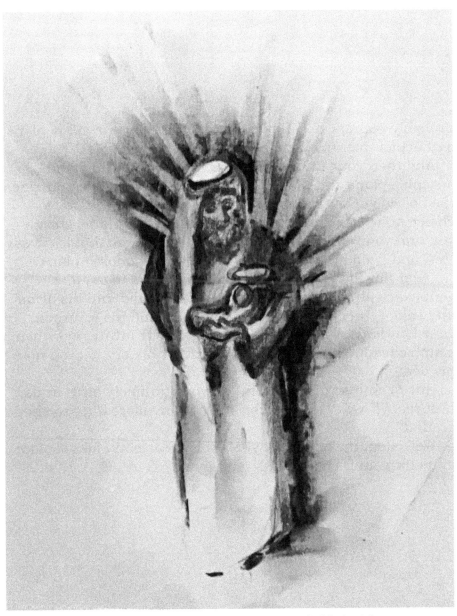

Joseph, bless his heart, took your child into his arms.

Joseph

We don't know why, but we think Joseph had waited for Mary for a long time. We don't know why, but we think he was old and she was his wish coming true.

We think he probably planned and built a home for her before he ever knew who she was to be, and we think he probably planned a baby, too, in due time, to crown his plans and achievements by making a father out of him.

And then your future stirred and scrambled time and Joseph's plans and picked him up and sat him down outside the bounds of common decency and faced him with a choice no man should ever have to make: should he choose you and your child and his own humiliation, or should he say "No" and keep his honored place and time-honored plans?

"Fear not," the angel said to him and says to us, and gentle Joseph, bless his heart, took your child into his arms and said, "Mine, too," and put his honor and his future in your hands, and risked his life to save your future, and then simply disappeared, too unimportant for history to even note his death.

But we still struggle to fend off your untimely birth in us. "Not ready!" we say. "Not yet!" "Too many more days to shop around."

Well, God, make us ready! Make us fear not! Make a place in us for you! Be born in us anyway.

Your child would have been born somehow.

Angels and Wise Ones

No matter that the multitude of angels had rehearsed their song for an eternity. No matter that the wise ones were already in motion.

No matter that your child would have been born somehow, sometime, somewhere, so persistent is your love for your world, dear God.

If Mary hadn't found it in herself to say, "Let it be for me as you say," it wouldn't have happened that way, or then, or there in Bethlehem of Judea, so little among the clans of Judah.

But it would have happened.

This is the thing that frightens us and humbles us and convicts us, and undeservedly ennobles us. For even though all history doesn't hinge on our yesses and on our nos, this little bit of history that you've given into our care does.

So, lead us gently, we pray, down into the Bethlehem of our hearts. Let it be for us as you say.

We have our manger ready.

A Fine Time to Come

You picked a fine time to come, dear God, in this season marked for us by terror, tragedy, and sadness.

Always, there is this wish in us and this requirement: that your coming should be an ending of the things that wound us, because the woundings cry out your absence to us and our abandonment.

We still expect the mighty King of the Clouds coming to take our pain away and don't expect, even though we know this story by heart, to find you here already in the midst of our pain, and so gentle.

You picked a fine time to come, because what your gentle coming now means for us is maybe not less pain but more—not necessarily, but maybe.

As long as we could think you stood above it all—inflicting here, saving there, making a list and checking it twice to find out who's naughty and nice—as long as we could think all that, then we could think that, being saved, we could stand above it all, too, with no more pain.

You picked a fine time to come. Now we don't know what to think, what to wish for.

If you should, truly, love the world so much you'd give your child, your Self, into the midst of the world's anguish, what does it mean for us, and what should we do? Does our pain cry out, in fact, your presence and not your absence?

Here's the dawning, fearful, joyful thing we think we begin to see.

If you hadn't made the world for love, we wouldn't hurt so much.

If you didn't dwell in love in the world, neither would you.

But, how terrible it must have been for you without a world to love. There would be no pain but also no joy. No love but only loneliness. We would take you in our arms to soothe the memory of it.

We've been lonely, too.

You've picked a fine time to come! We have our manger ready, and there'll be lots of presents. You'll love the tree.

The sheep will keep.

Shepherds

No more for the shepherds than for us, dear God, were angels an everyday thing. And for them, like for us, angels sang the end of things at the same time they sang the new beginning of things.

There's something about this season we set our jaws against. We start to clench up long before we ever set foot in a store, and not just because we've been through it all so many times before. It's the past we guard ourselves against.

And when angel stories first start to stir in us, we think we'll only hear the angels hectoring, "Why did you do this? Why did you not do that? You have done those things you ought not to have done. You have not done those things you ought to have done!"

But angels never ever sing the past. Angels always only sing the future—not the distant future like we think the prophets sing and not the future merely stretching out the present.

Angels sing the future coming at us with a question, and we are sore afraid because we never hear good will towards us in that singing, never hear your pleasure with us in it, never hear you whisper, "Will you come to Bethlehem with me and see what I am doing now, see who I am being now?"

We never hear you ask us, "Will you do what I am doing with me, now? Care for whom I'm caring now, care with me for whom I care for, now?"

Dear God, this time let the angel songs silence the accusations and send us to Bethlehem to attend your birth among us. The sheep will keep, because they also are kept in you.

CHRISTMAS

Christmas Eve

Finally, we are gathered around the place of your birth. Everything that would be new and good in us and around us gathers us wishing, yearning, hoping, straining to be born with you.

Everything old and bad in us and around us—disease, fear, rage, lust, greed, envy, pride, despair, bitterness, grudge—gathers, too, hoping to be healed, hoping to quiet this newborn hoping that only sharpens our pain, as we fail to see that it is the pain of you being born among us and within us.

How can it be that even when you come gently and touch first everything in us that loves babies and wants to hold and cuddle and soothe and feed—how can it be that even then, even now, this old rage rises up to strike you down?

But everything that would be new and good in us and around us also has its own yearning strength, and we cheer you on as you brave the dangers of our new birth, elude the threats and the deeds of the Herod in us, find a safe place to hide from us in the midst of our oldest enemy, Egypt, and return young and strong to outwit even our wisest wisdom and our best good, lead us on to lure out the disciple in us—and even the apostle.

And then—and we still don't understand this, and still don't quite believe it—you turn and take into your embrace everything that fears in us and everything that rages and everything that dies in us, and you die of it, and it dies, too. Even our death dies as your death dies, too.

You see—and we know you see because you've been through it—it's because we can't see and can't quite believe the end of it all that this beginning around which we gather tonight frightens us so much even as it fills us with hope.

And, as everything that would be new and good in us gathers you in our arms to hold and cuddle and soothe you, gather us also in your arms and calm our fear and give us, with your care, the courage to see this new life through with you, in Jesus's name, born this day.

Alleluia!

The Love Child Is Born.

Christmas Day

Once again, the love child is born. Once again, the peace child is born. One again, the hope child. Once again, the joy child.

Unfamiliar alleluias are on our lips, and we thank you, dear God, for the child and for the alleluias, all so strangely born.

But, what child is this?

What plot is this against our resignation, against our apathy, against our unhappiness, against our business as usual that we should be yearly lured, wooed, seduced into bearing in our hearts the pain of the birth of love and peace and hope and joy, and on our lips the agony of the birth of alleluias?

What world is this where cradle and cross, birth and pain, love and pain, peace and pain, hope and pain, joy and pain should be so tightly bound together?

This is the question that our lives shape. This is the question that shapes our lives. To which your answer always and only is the birth pangs of the love child, the peace child, the hope child, the joy child, by which our lips are always strangely shaped for alleluias.

Three kings, maybe four whisper and tickle their camels.

Wise Ones

Grim and wrath scurry into dark corners to hide from the sound of your laughter, dear God.

Abraham and Sarah look at each other and twinkle knowingly. Elizabeth and Zechariah hold each other's sides against the onslaught of mirth they know will come.

Trees normally and always green burst into baubles and strings of handmade things while other trees without a by-your-leave bend and bow and crack cold joints at the do-si-does whistling through their branches.

Sheep sprout wings, we swear, and bleat and then sing alleluias, sending shepherds tumbling and somersaulting into Bethlehem.

Three kings and maybe four whisper and tickle their camels into a gallop. They already knew, as camels always seem to do.

Herod's throne trembles and then begins to dance while Herod hangs on for dear life, and the Herod in us quavers between hope and fear. And a cuckoo—we swear! No—an angel flies circles around Joseph's head, nudges him in the ribs, whispers in his ear until he does a little dance himself and then stands beaming beside Mary, who only smiles.

For now, you laugh, Jesus, at us and our oldness and our fear, and the round and repetition of our year breaks open like an egg. And the world is new! And we are new! And we laugh alleluias back atcha.

After Christmas

Now, step by step, the story of yourself among us begins to unfold again, familiar to us as our own life story or even more familiar, lost as we so often are in our own life stories.

We are caught between yawn and wonder at it: the story of Emmanuel, God with us, told now more than two thousand times in church-measured years, in danger always of becoming just an old, old story unreasoning our being here to tell and hear it all again.

Yet something always breathes in it and sometimes burgeons and sometimes breaks forth to seize us by our yawns and transform them into wonder—or wondering.

We wonder, dear God, what unfathomable passion draws you to and through Mary to be at our side? And who was she and who are we that this should be?

We preen, search for secret virtues, and vainly seek to set ourselves apart from chimpanzees and goldfish, but can't believe the simpler truth, that the desire that drives us to find ourselves in you also drives you to find yourself in us!

The crazy truth is, we are more comfortable with condemnation and loneliness than with your reasonless love. "See?" we say as we sin to break your love's embrace. "It cannot be. It must not be true!"

Then, once again you don human flesh and human face and human joy and human pain to say two thousand times two thousand times, "But it is."

What can we say to that?

How can we answer but with thanks and praise, two thousand times two thousand times?

EPIPHANY

January

Each year, you and we conspire together to tease each other with talk of new beginnings, dear God. In the year's deepest gathering dark, we speak words of a new year when nothing we see or hear around us hints of newness.

Into the deepest gathering darkness of ourselves, where nothing suggests newness except our yearning for newness, you speak yourself among us: swaddled Emmanuel fleeing to some Egypt, narrowly escaping our love of darkness and fear of newness—cross-bound, rising Son, alleluia.

Why do we tease ourselves with awakenings when we might sleep our lives away? Because dreams subvert our sleep and betray us to our yearning. Because the year does turn and flings Spring at us just when we've learned to love Winter. Because life is strong as death, and we taste the bitterness of the healing of the grieving to which we cling.

We love and hate that you won't let us sleep and die. We give thanks and no thanks for your ever new self-stirring among us and within us.

And if we could bring ourselves to pray, it would be for the transformation of our hate and fear into the very fiber of love and our no thanks into strong harmonies for our songs of thanksgiving.

We seek a home. You give us a journey.

Who Are You?

Who are you, God, Really? Great master string puller? Puppeteer of the world? Source and solution of all our problems? Clockmaker? Clockwinder? Clockwatcher? Timekeeper? Bookkeeper? Nitpicker?

Legislator? Prosecutor? Judge? Advocate? Defendant? Victim?

Grandfather? Grandmother? Our sister? Our brother? Our husband? Our wife? Our lover? Real regular guy or gal? Naked, hungry beggar just out of jail and at our door?

Comedian of the world? Parabler of the universe? All of the above? None of the above? World's surprise sunrise? We pursue you from image to image. You pause to feed us with each one, and then, daring us to follow, you dance away.

We cry, "Who are you, really?" You cry, "Who are you, really?"

You are more than we bargain for—and less. We seek a home. You give us a journey. So make us fit for the journey.

Be, if need be, the one we pursue and the one who pursues us, but also be, we pray, as you have always been, our companion and guide.

We watch Jesus call.

Why Do We Gather Here?

Why do we gather here, dear God, except out of a sense it's somehow important that we do?

When the right things are going on, we can maybe say why it's important to us, although often enough it escapes us even then.

What's harder to figure out is why it should be important to you. We're so small in the scheme of things.

We suppose it's partly a matter of which scheme of things we're thinking about. When we consider the lilies like Jesus told us to do once, we come off better. But there are precious few lilies in January—just this white expanse of space and time and leafless trees, and our memories are short.

It's why we're so baffled and entranced as we watch Jesus again call those fishermen. There's nothing we can see about them to make them stand out from a hundred others tending nets that day.

Why did he call them? Why did they follow him? What did they think they could have or do? We think that if they only thought he was important they'd have stayed home, watched him on TV.

To take off like they did, they must have thought they were important.

From here, we know how right they were if they did, because from here they're history and not just dead. But they weren't history then. So, how'd they know?

Do you see what we're asking here, dear God? Who are we that you should be mindful of us who watch history only on TV? And why do you constantly call us who feel you calling mostly only in our yearning?

It's our yearning, of course, that gathers us here. What's hard for us is keeping in mind that our yearning is itself already an answering to your calling.

We should be praying not so much for answers to all these questions ahead of time, but for the shaping of our answering yearning for the loving and serving of the world you love so much.

A blue jay huddles in the bottom of a bush.

February

This weather is dour and changeable. Winter, embarrassed by its performance so far, holds its breath, not knowing whether to blow cold or warm, then blows both hot and cold. Confused Winter, forgetting where February was folded up and put away, blows March winds and rains by mistake.

Quiet for once, a blue jay huddles in the bottom of a bush and braces for whatever comes next. A concerned cat, hurrying past seeking shelter from uncertainty, doesn't see its breakfast shivering there. And we, too, turn south seeking sun and north seeking snow as we try to escape this day you have made for us to rejoice and be glad in.

O God, you give us this day and no other, so teach us to love this day. Free us from our yesterdays and our tomorrows and from the greener grass and deeper snow elsewhere. For today there are neighbors to love and be loved by, mourners to comfort and be comforted by, sick people to heal and be healed by, imprisoned ones to visit and be freed by, naked people to clothe and be warmed by.

All are one, and we are one in Jesus Christ, through whom we give you thanks and praise.

The Power of Our Refusal

We are born clinging, dear God, and all our lives are a
reluctant learning of letting go. Enduring monuments to the
power of our refusals populate even the long silences of our
sleeping.

Yet, while our nights persist, our days go by, each one
deftly and faithfully eluding our clinging, undermining
our refusals, offering themselves one by one for our new
embracing, working at our clenched fingers and saying, "Go,"
and opening your arms and saying, "Come." You are in the
middle of each one of them.

And at what cost to you?

Do you, also, suffer our refusing-clinging and the time
between our letting-go and our returning-embracing?
And does the cross that haunts our lives and breaks our
grasping-clinging also haunt yours?

The refusal in us demands that it should not be so—that
you should instead stand unmoving and unmoved and thus
be God for us. Teach us, we pray, in the passion of Jesus,
that the passion and pain of your love for us is like the
passion and pain of our love for our own children, and thus
be God for us.

You Came to Capture Us

In the first ice-blue dawning, the shapes of our surroundings get lost in black shadows. As you horizon us with light, dear God, darkness clings and hides on this side of things, and we hide, too, and cling to the dark, our arms embracing nothing and holding it to ourselves.

In the noonday of your presence, color captures our darkness, and the emptiness in our arms fills, and even our hiding is in you, and our clinging is in your embrace.

You are the source of our greatest fear and the object of our greatest anger. How can we escape you? You are the fulfillment of our deepest wish, the lost lover of our souls. How can we come to you?

When we flee from you, you are there to hide us. When we seek you out to claim you for our very own, you dance away to lead us on and to make us your very own.

We can't escape you, and we can't capture you. We can only give you thanks and praise in Jesus's name, in whom you came to capture us.

LENT

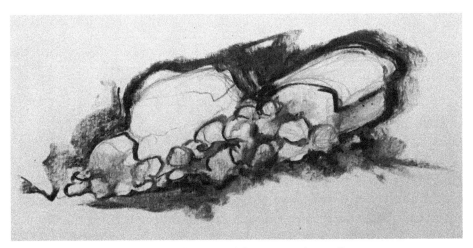

Why not bread from a stone?
March and the Truth of Spring

Now it's Lent, and we would follow you into the wilderness of your chosen suffering—not the suffering of our martyrdom that chooses to suffer rather than to love, but yours that suffers as a consequence of choosing to love . . .

We would follow you into your wilderness of your chosen suffering, but we are mystified that you should be tempted in your wilderness by what you already have.

If you could make a universe from nothing by speaking a word, why not bread from a stone? We fail to see the deviltry in this.

Why not rule the nations? Gods do that. Why not jump from the tallest buildings and not get hurt? Gods don't suffer and die!

Maybe you don't realize how important you are to us—you, safe harbor for our dearest wishes—so, if you should hunger and wonder and die, what about our wishes?

Your vast invulnerable aloneness, your having all things in the palm of your hand, your omnipotence that can love without losing—what about all that if you should hunger and wonder and die?

We are both enthralled and enraged that you should choose to love and, thus, to die. And so we pray that in your dying, our rage might die, too, and we might be finally freed to follow you and choose to love, and thus to die.

Eating Our Own Words

We eat our own words often enough, dear God, and when they are words of woe, we are thankful enough to eat them. But when we are called to eat your Word and drink your life and thus to know in the depths of our bodies and our very souls the woe that the sickness and the sadness and the injustice and the terror of this world you love so much causes you, we cry, "Whoa! Enough! We can't bear it!"

We can't bear to know in the depths of our bodies and our souls that the things for which we are always most thankful, the things we desire the most from you—your loving healing presence in all the times and places of our lives—that all of it means also pain for you and woe and lament for you who suffer the pain of our pain, the sadness of our sadness, the injustice of our acts of injustice.

How can we bear not only our own pain but also yours?

But you bear this pain, too, and bearing it, you make our bearing of it possible and our giving thanks, for in Jesus Christ, your child, your very self, you have borne our flesh and its agony and its joy, and in Jesus Christ, our brother, our very self, we have borne your flesh and its agony and its joy.

And for that reason, it is in his name that we give you thanks and praise.

You begin your walk to Jerusalem.

Singer of the Springtime

The planets and our calendars and our thermometers all coincide to sing Spring, dear God, so why do our bodies and our souls still shiver Winter? We think it is not just our nerve endings that shiver us but some far deeper thing. Why is it you must die so we, too, might sing Spring?

We stumble, and even the world's weather will hesitate, so steeped are we, like Abrahams and Sarahs, in our oldness. How can we, who have spent our power, bud, and flower and bear your promise?

Dear God, we can learn to love Winter and death, but we cannot bear your promising! For it is finally your promising that measures us and not your law, which would be easier.

And now once more you begin your journey to Jerusalem and bid us follow, to wallow in tired hosannas and feast and sleep and betray and deny and watch our oldness die, and struggle against the resurrection of our souls and bodies.

We pray for courage in the name of Jesus, singer of your Springtime, who taught us also to sing your Spring's Kingdom.

Seeds sprout in warm windows.

Spring's Kingdom

It is as if time had tilted, O God. Hours and days begin to slip and slide and tumble over one another as they rush to storm Spring's kingdom.

And we storm, too, our skin storming for sun and warmth and color, our seeds sprouting in warm windows, straining and pressing against the glass, wishing our houses around for more sun and more, our plows and spades and hoes trembling and beginning to glow at the prospect of the warm, wet earth's overturning.

And you storm, too, dear One—you will laugh at least one more snow storm at us, and we will slip and slide and tumble over one another and fumble in closets for stored Winter clothes and toys and stashed Winter thanksgivings.

In March, dear God, we have to laugh our thankfulness or we would surely turn surly and cry. But you know that, so we laugh you our thanks for March and for your laughter and for the way they humble and toughen our hoping,

We know that, having laughed us March and Jesus, now you will cry us Good Friday and death and life anew, your Spring kingdom's straight gateway.

HOLY WEEK and EASTERTIDE

Born Into Love

We don't know how to love you, Dear God. Since the days of our birth when you first aroused us from sleep and maybe before, you have also aroused us to love. That has been the fact of our lives, our deepest joy, our greatest pain.

We were born into love with our mothers and fathers, and while there may have been a time when their love was enough and good enough, we don't remember it. We remember in our bones not enough and too much and the rage to have more and the bitter, brave, necessary renunciations never quite accomplished.

Love, they say, slept a while when we were children, but in fact we fell in love with the world. We loved it with our eyes, our noses, our ears, our skin, our hands, our feet, our muscles, and learned, then, not to want to die for fear of losing the world.

If life had ended then or been suspended, we would have been okay, but love lured us on, drove us on. Puppy love, they said and knew they lied, while for us the world we loved disappeared. Then we thought we would rather die than not have that loved one, and we thought we could die for that loved one, until we finally chose and were chosen by the one for whom we felt we could live.

It wasn't enough, of course, although we didn't really know it then, because the world reappeared in the emerging real flesh, real blood, real person of our loved one, of our babies, of our houses and cars and pickup trucks, and of the work and play of our bodies and minds. And we loved them all and learned again not to want to die and lose the world we loved, and learned we would and learned, or so we thought, not to love so much so we wouldn't lose so much and hurt so much.

But it's not enough. There's still this love that complicates our lives and makes us pray, and it threatens always to turn our want to greed and lust and envy, our work and play to desperate busyness, our angers into hatred.

This love's for you, this love that confuses us so by going beyond anyone or anything we might have or own. We know it in our bones, and we pray so as to bring it to mind. This love's for you, and we don't know how to love you or love the world you love so much you give your child—your self— to live and die and rise again, to love and lose and die and eternally rise again.

How can we pray except to give you a great thanksgiving as complicated as the lives we lead with you in love, and pray you'll always lead us on and lure us out to love and teach us as you lead us on how to love you?

You mount your child, yourself, on that donkey.

Palm Sunday

When you mount your child, your very self, on that donkey and ride down over that hill and through the valley of our dry bones and up through the Golden Gate walled off against your coming, some wild thing surges in us that sends cries of "Hosanna!" and "Crucify!" struggling for space in our throats and on our lips.

At last! This is the end of waiting and working, the end of endless talking. The best we've always wished for has come.

The worst we've always feared has come.

And then you sweep the temple clean and curse the fig tree and tell us we can do it, too, and even move a hill from here to there. Our hearts exult. We are four years old, and Superman is coming true.

But why, then, this crucifying? And why this dying —this thing that super gods and supermen don't do?

We draw our super swords to fend off the awful truth that bends and breaks our minds and hearts. And when you stay our hand, we slip away and sulk and say we do not know you. Because, in truth, we suddenly do not know you.

Draw, we pray, our bent and broken swords and our wounded minds and hearts to and through this death of yours to life we've never known before.

That Donkey That Always Stands Ready

Year after year, dear God, you climb onto that donkey who always stands ready to bear our hopes for us, borrowed from the one who always stands ready to let his donkey do the bearing and you do the riding. And, year after year, we come out to wave our palms and cheer you on, choose Barabbas, crucify you, and cluck our tongues at those silly, ragged few who, despite themselves, see the Resurrection in it all. And then we wander away wondering why we let ourselves in for all this again and again and why you do.

The thing of it is—the pain of it is—that every time, in between the cheering and the choosing, and before the crucifying, we really hope! The future opens just a crack and allows us to think that maybe it'll be different. Our life, we mean, and not just this story.

Maybe this time we'll catch on to what's really going on and break loose from the cheering, crucifying crowd and risk the lonely path from the courtroom of judgment to the courtyard of derision. Flitting from shadow to shadow to Golgotha to witness, this time, the crucifixion of the One we love and who loves us and somehow finally see and know, despite ourselves, the Resurrection in it all and life made new.

It's this hope and the pain of it we hold you responsible for, what we try you for and find you guilty of and flog you for. This hope is why we crucify. Because this hope you rouse in us is not at all what we've always wished for. We've wanted saved, we've wanted rescued from our lives, from the good and bad of them, the aging and dying of them.

But the hope you rouse in us calls us to the very center of all this, offers us our lives anew as a work to do, a cross not just to bear passively but to take up and carry faithfully because that's what you do: carry the cross of our lives, faithfully.

This hope is what we can't forgive you for. We want you off in glory land, and we want to be there, too, and we crucify you to get you out of the center of our lives and get you back to heaven where you belong. Can you forgive us for this? For refusing the gift of our lives made new over and over again? For saying no to the Resurrection in it all?

This hope you rouse in us when you climb on the donkey, this hope that gives us such pain while promising such joy, this hope knows you can and will, and it's this hope in us that gives you thanks and praise.

Maundy Thursday

Palm Sunday confused us again, dear God. We were caught up in our love of parades, and we sang hosannas, and meant hosannas. And yet we knew betrayal was in the air and that our hand was in it and that your hand was in it. We don't know why we let ourselves be set up year after year and day by day and let our children be set up. And we don't know why you allow yourself to be set up, your child to be set up.

Year after year and day by day, you mount your donkey and lure out our wishfulness, spawned by desire and fear and rage, and we form it into cries of "Christ!" and "Crucify!" Day by day, year after year, we cry "Christ" and lure you onto your donkey and onto your cross.

What has to die before love can arise? And why must it always be you who dies and we who put you to death? And can we sing hosannas for that? For all these reasons, we resist your coming. And yet we say "Come!" Ride roughshod again and again on your donkey into our hearts.

Golgotha looms on your spring's horizon

Good Friday

What a wonder it would be, dear God, if sun and skin and calendar should all sing Spring in unison. What praise if Winter pallor should suddenly turn pink. What awe there would be at air that kisses but doesn't bite. Then, thanksgiving would spring to our lips and flow naturally into song.

Why, then, does the waiting not end? What wind is this that still blows chill? What horse thief hangs in our family tree that sets it apart from the sugar maple and gives its sap the taste of vinegar?

Why must you suffer our Winter before we can enjoy your Springtime?

Golgotha looms on your Spring's horizon with a lonely tree, but we would rather embrace a maple and its sweetness than that tree and its gall. So we cry, "No! You must not!" so that we might not.

But you embrace that tree for us and pay the price for our Springtime, and we still don't understand, but we find our hearts full with your love and our unworthiness, and our thanksgivings overflow anyway.

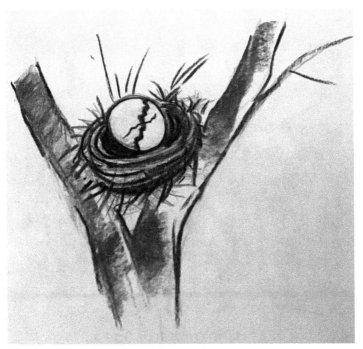

An odd egg lies hatching.

Easter Egg

What an odd egg lies hatching in this Easter nest you've woven with us, dear God. This Resurrection of yours answers no questions, solves no problems, fulfills no heart's desire, simply sits hatching.

What secret peeps from this torn inner sanctum of fertility?

What queer bird comes ever forth?

We come here with wounds to heal, consciences to salve, fears to allay, beauty and strength to celebrate and sanctify, and you answer with this Resurrection that turns tombs to wombs—to give birth to what?

This fertile emptiness repels us and lures us, frightens and invites us, disappoints us, empties us, and fills us with the wildest hoping, sending us out to say "What?" to our friends and even to our enemies? That you are so fruitfully and fertilely not here, that we are more preciously here than we've ever been before?

What an odd thing. Alleluia!

The rock split open.

Time Had Grown Too Tired

It seems like time had grown too tired to hold back the tide of eternity. The rock that guarded the day against the dark split open and disgorged the dead to walk among the living. The veil that guarded the day against the light was torn in two, but no avenging angel stepped forth. There'd only been that three-day silent dark.

And then, the women who went to try to give some smell and semblance of life to death saw that death had only killed what death can kill and were sore afraid. They, like us, knew what to do with death, but here was life all new standing there in front of them.

We would have thought that the great unmaking and the making of all things new would be more a matter of strobe lights and trumpets and crashing cymbals than this teasing of weeping women in the garden and men on the road to nowhere and breakfast at the beach.

But of course, it is you who are risen and not some creation of our wildest wishing. We were fooled for a moment by the donkey, but now we see, and don't see, but we give you thanks and sing Alleluias!

You fooled us by filling our net with fish.

Sin Sits in Us Like a Spider

Sin sits in us like a spider, dear God, spinning its web. Sometimes we seem to remember flying free, enjoying the sun, enjoying ourselves, seeking a shady corner, and suddenly finding ourselves caught, struggling, enmeshing ourselves even more with our efforts to break free, then resting in our fetters, waiting for the spider to stride down the web to wrap us up, finish us off—who never comes, who simply sits smiling, while we struggle again, entangling ourselves even more.

Sometimes it seems we've broken free, tasting freedom, flying up again past the smiling spider but with one strand still sticking around our ankle, slowing our flight as it stretches, maybe to break, then snapping us back, snarling us again in our struggles to be free.

Sometimes it seems we've been here forever, born into this web we hate and love. Looking out over its creation and smiling how good it is, the spider seems so satisfied with what it's spun.

It isn't good, God. The freedom we remember and the freedom that we've tasted even in our fettered flight says it isn't good at all!

Sometimes, we must confess, we've thought the spider was you. Sometimes in our struggles, we've spun a god to save us from our web and found we'd only spun another smiling spider. Sometimes in our failed flight, we've caught a breath of wind, an updraft catching us to stretch the strand that held us down.

Once, we know, we saw you striding freely down the web and then become enmeshed with us, caught at the crossing of two strands, and saw the spider strike like lightning to enshroud you in an even finer, stronger web. We struggled over to where you lay and found you gone, escaped! And we know we saw, up in the corner where the spider lurked, an empty spider shell, a vacant spider smile.

You wouldn't believe what happened next if you hadn't seen it, and we know you did and that you laughed and laughed with love and sadness.

We panicked! We thought, "Who will tend the web? Who will spin?" and set ourselves to spinning: "A net for fishing," we said, although it was ourselves we meant to catch for fear of flying free.

But you fooled us by filling our net with fish and feeding us and convicting us three times of loving you and sending us flying freely off to feed your sheep.

Thanks!

Easter Is Come and Gone

Winter is in retreat, we're pretty sure, and we give you thanks and praise for that. But we have to say it seemed for a while like it was retreating backwards with wind and wet and white streaming in to keep this place cold. This bright day has the color of warm, but even if it doesn't have the feel of warm, our eyes conspire with memory and hope to create Spring even so.

Easter's come and gone, and we give you thanks and praise for that, but resurrection's been a matter of the eye and the imagination and the heart's hoping, but our bodies are still cold. It is only with fear and trembling that we pray for the warming and enlivening of our heavy bodies, because dreaming and hoping is one thing, but doing is another.

Our enlivened minds may see the shape of your kingdom, our enlivened imaginations add color to it, but our enlivened bodies must be your kingdom's flesh and blood and do its work, and we are lazy and afraid. But you have given us your flesh and your blood, so how can we not offer you ours for the warming and the doing?

So enliven us, we dare to pray. Breathe your breath into us. Fill us with your Spirit for the doing of your kingdom.

SPRING and PENTECOST

A bird flew into our barn.

Ascension Day

A bird flew into our barn the other day, dear God. We don't know what kind it was except that it wasn't a chickadee, because if it were, it wouldn't have panicked the way that bird did when we walked in. The barn doors were wide open, but we forgot for a while that we were standing there. We were so involved in the plight of the bird that we didn't see our part in it.

She could see daylight and the pine woods through the window at the back, but she knew nothing of glass or sin or how you can't necessarily fly through what you can see through. She kept fluttering against what she couldn't see and didn't understand. Then she'd back up and fly at it as hard as she could. We were afraid she'd hurt herself and moved closer to try to help and scared her more.

Once, she got where the light was just right and saw herself in the glass. She stopped somehow in mid flutter and spread her wings in such a way that we didn't know whether she was saying, "Help me! Help me!" to her reflection or "Don't come in! You can't get out!" or both.

And then she started to fall and went back to her frantic fluttering.

That was when we came to our senses and remembered we weren't the bird struggling to get free but we were the problem, for all our sympathy and wanting to help. So we left. And as we walked up to the house, we thought of you and how hard it must be to set free things free.

We turned to watch the bird fly out of the barn door and saw, for a moment at least, why you came to us in Jesus but also why you left, and why you come and go continually and why we catch a glimpse of you only just before and just after our moments of flying free.

We loved you then, and, remembering, we love you now.

Bread and grape juice lie broken and spilled.

Communion at Pentecost

O God, you are God in all places and in all times.

We are a people in confusion, living in the midst of one of time's turnings.

Christ, our older brother, is gone. With wisdom, he pointed out for us the good and evil and the height and depth of things. In his place is a competition of voices, wishes, dreams, fears, seductions, memories, and wild hopes, not yet Spirit, not yet advocate, not yet comforter, only this groaning.

Bread and grape juice lie broken and spilled in front of us, the bread threatening to be just bread, the juice halted in its journey to wine, the wine in its migration to blood.

Fill us with your Spirit, we pray. Transform this bread of our lives into your living flesh, this juice into your blood, this brokenness and spilledness of ours into new life, these groanings of ours into truth-telling.

Turn the tables on our time, dear God, fill its emptiness with your presence. Order its chaos, inform it with your eternity in Jesus's name.

ORDINARY TIME

Your spring presents a spectacle of new growing.

March and April were a Gnawing Fear

We wonder again, O God, at your Spring spectacle of new green growing. Winter trees and vines sleep so deeply that they hint and threaten death to us. Were it not for the maple syrup, March and April in New England would be a gnawing fear that life is made for death and not for life. All that was dead or tended towards death in us trembled in late Winter winds.

But all that is past. What seemed dead around us now bursts forth with life, and all that is alive in us or tends towards life trembles and flutters in May winds and bursts into hope and songs of praise and the possibilities of love.

We were awakened in the night by the strong sound of wind, and at first, we were afraid until we thought, "O yes, that strong sound is the sound of leaves blowing, and that wind speaks of life and life abundant.

Dear God, though thanksgiving springs to our hearts and lips almost unbidden, it doesn't come unmixed, for your Springtime's seeming easy greening shows up the sluggishness of our own new growing. We don't know whether trees resist their new leaves and seek to stay asleep, but we do know something strong in us would rather sleep and die.

And it is that strong dying in us, most of all, that we offer up to you for healing on this May day. In Jesus's name, in whose dying, dying died.

Love seeds and sprouts in our hearts.

Is This the Winter that Will Not End?

O God, what is it in us that, when we plant a seed, we're so sure it won't sprout and grow and is so surprised, over and over again, when it does?

What is it that whispers, "This is the Winter that will not end, the year no leaves will come, no green at all. I knew it all along"?

What is it in us that, when the Winter does end, loves Winter better and feels betrayed and abandoned when even the seeds that we have planted sprout and grow towards fruit and death, leaving us behind?

What is it in us that can't believe that the love that turns the year and drives the seasons and grows the green and exults in the fruit and enfolds the death loves us also and exults in us and enfolds us, too?

Is it for this in us, this battered, bitter, frightened child, you give your child, dear God? If that is so, then we must see Spring differently and feel the echoes of the songs and high callings in the treetops singing also in ourselves.

How can we give thanks for it? What songs are there that can sing and speak the love that seeds and sprouts in our hearts? And what deeds of love might we do, speaking volumes louder than our words or songs?

As you love us, dear God, also lead us.

Lilacs guard the doorway to summer.

Lilacs

Now, God, lilacs guard the doorway to Summer, lingering so as not to lose the light sweetness and lacework promising of springtime when anything might be or be made new. Only we and the ash trees are reluctant to pass through. Everything else rushes in and on to definition and fruition.

We and the ash trees hang back because the passage from the hinting of leaves to leaves, from the airy teasing of blossoming to the heavy finality of fruit, from the promising to the being and the doing, from word to flesh, dares dying.

We and the ash trees hang back and linger in our blossoming until our promising passes on into mere memories of promises. What-might-be becomes wistful what-might-have-been without passing through the heavy, final, fruitful, birthing, being, doing, and dying.

But, ah, God, you do demand fruit from us and a daring of dying, and we are afraid.

Yet you, yourself, have borne the fruit and dared the dying so that we might bear and dare and not be so afraid. And we are ashamed, and we give you thanks as we and the ash trees step fearfully through the lilac door.

This budding, bursting, blossoming time still surprises us.

How Many Million Mays?

How many million Mays there must have been already, dear God, and still we are astonished? This budding, bursting, blossoming time still surprises us, still delights us, still twines itself in and around the bonds of our boredom, still insinuates itself in between us and our apathy, still teases the deadly repetitions of our days with the utter newness of your eternal returns.

Forgive us. Though we're very well taught that everything that is emerges from your grand aloneness, something deep and pagan in us suspects much more going on in this merry, Mary, marry month. For we are borne on May breezes, and lullabied in this new rustle of leaves, and bathed in the breath-warmth of this air, and surrounded and suckled in these sweet smells.

One moment in May hints of deep, divine secrets, and before June carries us off once more into forgetfulness, we offer praise, for in May we know that your Fathering of us roots in the deep soil of your Mothering of us.

We remember backward in order to see forward.

Memorial Day

This weekend of memories stands guard over all the summers of our lives like the grace that guards our mealtimes, bringing us to a halt before we plunge into the feast time of the year.

The time between our seed time and our own time has sometimes contained greatness, and remembering has been a cause for great pride.

But the time has also sometimes tarnished and diminished us, and remembering has been a matter of great pain.

Dear God, here's the source of the painfulness of remembering: if our memory's scanning should catch a glimpse of greatness, our own time feels diminished by comparison. But if our memory's scanning should not catch a glimpse of greatness, we are bereft of a hope of greatness.

For, finally, we remember backward in order to see forward, and we might just forget forward the gathering sense that some greatness might now be required. So, we pray, be with us now on this weekend of remembering so that we might come to remember who we are to be.

Speaking of Spirit

Sometimes when we speak of you as Spirit, we speak wistfully and wishfully that you who seem so distant might also be with us and in us as you were once, that you might touch us like you did once, or maybe more than once. And sometimes we speak hopefully, sensing something impending in us and around us.

Sometimes it's our pain subtly turning from crying "death" to us to crying "birth and life" that cries out also to newly name you Spirit. And sometimes someone else's pain reaches out to touch our shoulder when we've turned our back, and when we turn again to look and maybe touch the pain, we touch you, too, touching us, and name you Spirit.

And sometimes when our moans and groans, that mostly try to pass for words and truths, speak clearly and truly of us and you, we know you, Holy Spirit, speaking, too.

So, God, Holy Spirit, do what you do. Impend in us. Stir and speak in our pain and joy. Touch us with the pain and joy of others.

Transform our moans and groans into words and truths.

And then send us out to do the work of love you do in Jesus's name.

Now the Sun Has Come

We thought it would never come, this burgeoning, blossoming time.

The gray cold had infiltrated our lives and dampened down whatever in us passes for wings and makes for flying. But now the sun has come, and we, like those silly, ugly Southern birds, hang out to dry whatever in us passes for wings.

But what is it in us flies—or would, unweighted? And what is it weighs us down once Spring begins to sing and we're still earthbound?

Too many Winters, too many flightless Springs, too many fruitless Summers, too many fallen Falls.

We seek seasons that don't just accumulate to weigh us down, and we think that you will never come and whatever in us flies will never fly. But is this you, fluttering and struggling in our breasts?

And is it our stubborn, stratified, ossified souls that cling to the seasons so they'll only come and never go—no burgeoning blossoming, no fruit, no blazing glorious dying, no restoring sleeping—only this gathering, deadening, weighing down?

Then come, Holy Spirit! Fly us! Break the bonds that we have forged with Winter and soar us! Glide us! Loop de loop us! Barrel roll us! Fly us!

You have dreamt and willed a rose to be.

You Grow Us

O God, just as you grow this new green around us, so do you grow us. Just as you have dreamt and willed a rose to be through ages and stages unimaginable to us and a rose has arisen, so have you dreamt and willed us. And though we, too, have passed through ages and stages unimaginable to us, we suddenly appear here to ourselves almost full grown but not quite finished.

It seems from where we stand that you have given your whole dreaming and willing into the beginnings of roses and that roses pass with ease into an ending that is a fulfilling and a glorifying, but that you have given our beginnings only the beginnings of your dreaming and your willing and that you lure us on not only to fulfill but to share in your dreaming and willing of us.

You have given us over into our own hands, and we don't know what to make of ourselves, and we are often afraid, and we often don't do well, and we often complain.

But you have given us signposts toward our hope for our self-making, and you have given us over not only into our own hands, but also into each other's, and we are shaped in each other's hands by love and by its lack. More than that, you have given yourself into our hands, and your willing, dying self on our communion tables cries out that fact.

And most of all, your Resurrection and your living dying presence here among us shouts that, after all, and all in all, and through it all, we are in your hands. And we are overwhelmed with ourselves and with each other and with you! And we give you thanks and praise.

We have grasped creation like a shiny, red apple.

Present at the Creation

God of Wisdom, you were present at the creation, and you are the life and the form and the beauty of every living thing. We give you praise and thanks for all the ways that you are present among us.

You are in the order and constancy of nature. You are in the beauty and bounty of our world. You are in the daily dividing of day and night, the yearly yielding of Summer into Autumn, of seed-time into harvest. You are in the varied joys that each time and season brings, and we give you thanks for all that.

You are also in the disorder and inconstancy on the boundary between ourselves and each other, and You suffer with us the pains and sorrows that each time and season brings. And we struggle to also give You thanks for this.

We struggle to free ourselves from the wish and illusion that creation is complete, that everything should somehow fit smoothly together, that we should share no responsibility for the creation of order and constancy and beauty and harmony, that we might rest comfortably in Eden as passive receivers of bounty and balm.

Forgive us for our sin of laziness. Give us courage and strength to shoulder the burden of creation that you have given us and which we have grasped like a shiny red apple and have found we can't put down.

Your grace sings your presence in bird songs.

Grace Grins Grand Green Smiles at Us

Your seasons cycle toward their fullness. Your grace surrounds us, undergirds us, sings your presence in bird songs, grins grand green smiles at us, laughs riotous reds and yellows and blues at us, fills us up.

We are nearly overwhelmed, but not quite, because there is that in us also that Summer can't touch, that accumulates seasons and swallows up Summers, adding each to each like weights on a scale and subtracting each one from all the rest in an always declining grand total. It is this in us that ages and dies and fears each succeeding Summertime that we offer up to you for saving.

For in you nothing can be lost, and in you each Summer gathers all the Summers that ever were. In your hands, all the Summer times are held as present and not past. And each life gathers all the lives that have come before, and all are held in Your hands as present and not past.

Gather, we pray, everything in us that ages and dies and fears the Summertime, and transform it all into love for the living and for the singing of praise for the fullness and the fatness and the lushness of your Summertime presence among us.

Our Own Sort of Magic

We've worked our own sort of magic with grain and grapes to make this meal of you, O God. We've taught the seed to grow thirtyfold, sixtyfold, a hundredfold, impoverishing the farmers with our plenty, increasing the hunger of those who have not and those who have.

We've improved the good out of the flour and replaced it with our own kind of eternity. We've tramped the grapes and preserved their juice from fermentation and thus preserved our virtue.

This bread and this juice lie dead upon your table and still you live in them. Though we've done our best and worst to tramp you down and squeeze you out, this meal is still you!

We can't eat without eating you. We can't do harm without harming you. The cries of the hungry are your voice crying. The hunger in us is hunger for you. We can't escape you.

Since we can't escape you, Dear God, we pray that you would open us up to receive your presence in this meal and everywhere. Calm our fear, heal our hatred, fill our emptiness with yourself.

Transform our hearts and bodies for praise, and then send us forth with food and drink and you for those who hunger for food and for drink and for you.

Lost in the Middle of Our Lives

Dear God, when we find ourselves lost in the middle of our lives, we find ourselves calling out, "Where are you in the middle of our lives?" It's as if we could find you in the middle of our lives, we would be able to find ourselves in the middle of our lives. And we wonder whether it would work the other way. We wonder whether, if we could just find ourselves in the middle of our lives, we would find you there, too.

There are times when we have found ourselves lost very near home and have never felt more lost. Those are the times we're talking about, and the old joke occurs to us, "Well, we know where we are, right here!" But the world has suddenly become strange, and it's home that's lost. And it's just then we find ourselves calling out, "Where are you in the middle of our lives?"

There are also times when we are suddenly strangers to ourselves right at home in a world become all too oppressively familiar. Those are the times we're praying about, and those are the times when you have never seemed stranger. And we find ourselves calling out, "Who are you in the middle of our lives?" And we wonder whether, if we could just figure out who you are, we would also be able to figure out who we are. And we wonder whether it would work the other way.

In the middle of this muddle of our lives, your Jesus appears bearing the double burden in his body of knowing just who you are and just who we are, because he is you and he is us all at the same time!

And here's the thing we can't imagine: We can't imagine the pain of it, the agony of loving us both.

We've been lost for a long time in the middle of our lives but have not called your name seriously for fear that, if you should answer and show us who and where you are and who and where we are, we would have to suffer some great thing, bear some great burden.

We didn't know that it was love we would suffer or that you would suffer, too, for love.

Help us, we pray, to bear this burden and, borne by your love, to become bearers of your love in Jesus's name.

John 6

You are the bread, dear God, and you are the grape's juice. No more than those people who gathered to listen to you on that hillside do we understand half of what you mean when you say nor half of what we mean when we say, "You are the bread." Like them, we work day in and day out for bread that perishes, never stopping for even a moment for fear that's all the bread there is.

We tease ourselves. We've teased ourselves for centuries, and you've teased us, too, with little bits of bread and tiny little cups spread out here before us and you. Our children always want more because they understand it's just an appetizer.

We, on the other hand, have trained ourselves—constrained ourselves—to be satisfied for fear that it may be all there is, fearing that there might be plenty more where it comes from, fearing that it may be only Wonder Bread and Welch's, fearing it may be much more and not wanting to find out.

Because, look, dear God, we've spent a lot of time on those sunny hillsides made so anxious by the plenty that seemed to come from nowhere that we would storm heaven to seize you and make you king just to assure the supply. We are numbed to the truth that you already are king and that plenty is already always coming, always here.

We don't want to find out because, terrified of sinking, we've also spent plenty of time in stormy seas. We're strangely satisfied to sink, because that is what we always knew awaited us, and there you came, walking by to calm our fear and spoil our satisfaction.

And just when we would grab you and wrestle you into our boat to be sure it never sinks, we scrape bottom, "safe on the other side," as the old song says.

Most of our time we spend in silence grubbing for the daily bread that perishes as we think that, if this sacrament is only Wonder Bread and Welch's, then the silence is only silence and the bread that perishes is the only bread there is.

But if before us is the bread of Heaven, then the silence is yours! So we break our silence to take the dare to pray that the breaking and the giving and the taking of the bread and cup may mean the breaking of your silence for just one moment to tell us there is heaven even in the leaven of it.

Nourish us with bread and juice so that we may bear even the long silences.

We come together to celebrate our nation's birth.
Independence Day

God of all peoples and all nations, we come together before you on Independence Day to celebrate our nation's birth—not with unmixed mirth, for our love and pride have suffered wounds. Our love and pride are mixed with pain and yet remain love and pride, but chastened.

There is danger in our chastening that on this day we might not give thanks for the resiliency of liberty, though threatened; for the strength of this land that, in spite of greed and land lust, still buttresses us and inspires us and shames us with its beauty; for the long, slow, torturous birth of equality that still continues among us and, often enough, in spite of us; for the spark of greatness and nobility that smolders and slumbers in our hearts and flares forth always in the nick of time, or shortly thereafter; for the chastening of our love and pride that allows us to hope for an American rebirth on the birthday of America.

Thanks be to God. Thanks be to God. Thanks be to God.

We give you thanks that the wounds to our love and pride are self-inflicted, that there is no sterner judge of America than America, that our present pain is as much a gift of our forefathers and our foremothers and you as our liberty and our well-being to be tasted and trusted and savored and not to be thrust aside as something alien and undesirable.

Keep us ever watchful for meanness and fear that parade as economics and politics but seek victims and not justice. We ask your blessing and guidance for ourselves and for our leaders so we might renew what was begun so many years ago and we might finish our unfinished revolution.

The World around Us Grows Heavy with Child

O God of greenness and lushness, the world around us becomes heavy with child. Birth growth springs out around us and also summers in our souls. Seed—wind cast, bird cast, bee cast, and human cast—has been broadcast and has fallen.

First, fast, foolish path cast, rock cast, weed cast seed has sprouted and grown and goes. Weed seed grows still, but slows. Leaf, flower, and fruit of deep rich soil-cast seed grows fast, now, and flourishes, and we are filled with hope and come before you with praise and thanksgiving.

On the Fourth of July, we cast back worried glances at our seed days and wondered what, of all that was planted there and then, will come to fruit now. We have to confess that, in the hand full of good seed sown then and now, was also weed seed and sour grape seed and that, teeth on edge, we have fertilized and nurtured and harvested the one with the other.

We give you thanks that oaks and maples still stand. We confess that the elms and chestnuts are going and gone and that fast growing, fast living, fast dying poplars crowd our fields once carefully tended.

We lie fallow before your love, dear God. So plow us, harrow us, fertilize us, weed us, harvest us. Don't let your Word return to you unfulfilled.

We Pray Because We Want

We pray because we want, dear God. We rarely know what we want but we always know that we want. If we knew what we wanted, we probably wouldn't pray.

We might sing praises or cry laments for things that are finished, but we wouldn't pray with poising of pen and shaping of finger and tongue and teeth and lips and throat and heartstrings in hopes of hearing you speak to and give shape and meaning and direction to our wanting.

Such speaking is a straining to hear you speak what you want of us in our hopes that, if we only knew what you wanted, we might finally know what we want—the meaning of the moaning and groaning and stirring yearning that drives us to distraction and to pray.

We wouldn't pray at all if deep down we didn't know or hunch or gamble that such restless yearning that drives us to pray is a yearning for you and that it echoes your restless yearning for us!

We pray to open up a place in space and time where our restless yearnings might meet. And we speak to help create silence where we might hear you speak.

So speak, dear God, we pray. Emerge into our noisy silence that's the best we can do today. Merge our yearning into yours. Gather us into your purposes for us. Send us out to do the work you're working in us and in our world in Jesus' name.

It's difficult to discover the blessing in Japanese beetles.

The Blessing in Beetles

Dear God, we find it difficult to discover the blessing in Japanese beetles. There is an obvious sort of beauty shared by black widow spiders and rattlesnakes and gasoline floating on a puddle, but where's the blessing?

Just when grapevines and raspberry bushes and crabapple trees begin to do a kind of dance with the heavy gracefulness of expectant mothers met in a meadow to share their burgeoning promising, those brutal invaders appear, making piggyback promises of their own we'd just as soon not see.

Where is the blessing in beetles? Woodchucks and raccoons and deer are at least furtive. Even foxes aren't proprietary about our chicken houses. Rather do they sneak. But these country cousins of cockroaches act as if they own\ the place! And there's the rub: they don't even do us the justice of acting as if we trespass. It's just as if we don't even exist! Haven't they read Genesis? Don't they know who's been given dominion around here?

Ah. Now do we begin to see? Did you forbid the crabapple tree? Was our mother Eve too taken with the snake to see the beetle there, munching knowingly and sadly?

Is our story older than we know? Should we see not blessing in beetles but ourselves reflected in their iridescent, insatiable hungering? We shouldn't ask, because your answering is too weighty. Then, give us the strength to bear our brotherhood with beetles.

O God, your comings and goings among us are so subtle.

Baptism

O God, your comings and goings among us are so subtle and so secret. You slip into the back pew while we're busy singing your praises, and we almost don't notice you ease out the front door while we recess out the back.

And we don't quite see you standing around the fringes of our crowded coffee hour as you try to get a Word in edgewise. Or a glass of juice. Or a piece of cake.

Or standing along our street with your thumb out or sleeping in our sanctuary while we debate now and again whether to lock the doors but can never quite bring ourselves to.

Or crying from your wicker basket in our deacons' meetings as we wonder together what new shaping of space and time would best cradle your presence among us. Or wheedling yourself in your white dress somewhere in between our celebrations and our concerns and our intercessions and our great thanksgivings and our true confessions as you call our hearts out and elicit your new name, Kristia, from us and call forth promises from us we don't know whether we have the courage to make again and we're not sure we have the staying power to keep.

Yet, we suddenly discover ourselves meaning from the bottom of our hearts, "We do! We will! We'll really try!" We touch the truth of things, we who hold you in our arms, your kingdom coming as a child. We touch the love you bring all new to us and the love that you call forth from us.

Thanks! Thanks!

Where Are We?

Dear God, where, in this bundle of consequences that we are, are we? And where are you?

How do we sort ourselves out, and how do we sort you out from this welter of other people's hungers and other people's wishes that we are born out of and born into?

We emerge out of a wave of biology and history that began to roll before we ever were and will roll on as if we never were, most of us. We come to light as footnotes in other people's biographies, accidents of our parents' hungers. They hungered for each other, and they hungered for babies, but we were a surprise to them—and not always a pleasant one.

What a surprise it is for us to find ourselves alive daily, and, even more, to blame for our lives and for the lives of our children and for those of our neighbors.

And when we wind ourselves up to sort you out to blame for our lives—after all, you're the first cause of all these consequences, you from whose hunger everything emerges— you present yourself to us as blameless, the one who bears all the consequences!

And hidden in your blamelessness, we find our own foothold for a new, really first beginning for our lives, for which we would now gladly bear the blame and give you thanks and praise.

Goldenrod holds summer in the balance.

Goldenrod

Now, God, goldenrod holds summer in the balance holding green, withholding gold, fending off fruition, which is also dying. We are one with the goldenrod. And we hold our breath for fear of sneezing and sending summer tumbling into fruition, which is also dying.

If it were up to us, your kingdom would come in July, and eternity would be a contemplation of the anticipation of the celebration of the best apple, corn, and tomato crop ever but also a fending off of that fruition, which is also dying. Give us August courage, apple courage, corn courage, tomato courage which is the ending of the fending off of that fruition, which is also dying.

The Promise and the Cruelty of This Season

O God, we are caught between the promise and the cruelty of this season that now begins to totter toward its fulfillment and its ending. One side of us knows that we should know better than to be taken in again and again by this gathering green that now begins to go to the gold and red of fruition and also dying—the side of us that understands Winter only as the death of things and the deepest truth of things.

But there is that in us also that feels always the trembling under the snow and the rising warmth that keeps the freezing only a matter of surfaces and a saving of the seeds of things until just the right time—the side of us that gathers and gorges on the fruits of things and grows fat and sings praises.

We hear, dear God, and know you hear, the uncertainty in our singing and the faltering in our praising as that in us that dies or wishes to die rises up to be heard, too, and healed and brought back to life.

Sing, we pray, in our singing and in our deepest souls, the songs of your summertime, so that everything in us that lives or wishes to live and wishes life to all might flourish and bear good fruit.

Black-eyed Susans are the peaking of the blossoming.

Summer Seems to Pause

Summer seems to pause just now, dear God, giving us a moment to pause, too, and give praise for it. Black-eyed Susans are the peaking of the blossoming of the wildflowers of Summer. Now comes the Goldenrod, Fall's first flowering.

The early promises of our gardens have been kept and eaten. The lettuce is going to seed and the yellow squash is going to gold and gourd. Apples wink in the trees, and the relentless green of our tomatoes begins to mellow toward yellow. Corn pricks up its ears at the sound of omnivores salivating, the bears and the raccoons and the humans waiting.

And while we wait, we praise you for this Summer. God knows—you know—we have tried to complain about too much rain, and then it stopped—about the heat, and then you blew cool.

Our gardens laughed at us as they leapt at the sun that has now shined day after day, week after week of this, the only Summer they will have while we dip into our treasure trove of summers past for comparisons on which to found our complaints.

It may well be that the sun has shone pretty nearly every weekend, and the flowers are better than we can ever remember, but there were years when the blueberries were better.

There! We found the flaw to fend off the praise that wells up in our hearts. Just so do we demonstrate and confess how well-defended we are against the praise and just how hard you work to undo our defenses. The long, soft, warm evenings finally undo us in this Summer's pause, and so many unconnected to brutal days and sleepless nights. So we are without excuse and we must give you thanks.

How can we pray that, in addition to the Summertime, you would also give us the heart to praise. And yet we do, in Jesus's name.

O God, this table of yours speaks so many messages.

This Table of Yours

O God, bread of our lives, cup of our salvation, this table of yours speaks so many messages that we are confused by the expectations and fears and hopes that it arouses.

Your table speaks holiness, and we touch and taste the ways that we are not holy, dust and ashes in our mouths that make us speak our sin and thirst for the cup that never runs dry. Your table speaks of a meal, and it rouses the hunger in us that we have tried always to put aside because we despair of ever being filled—the hunger that saps all our other fulfillments.

These little bits of bread and tiny cups speak our fear that there is not enough, and yet proclaim that these small everyday bits and pieces are full of you—and are you, and we are given a vision of such plenty that out of our great hunger we sing thanksgivings beforehand and out of our fullness sing gratitude afterward.

Your table speaks especially that this hunger in us that we have tried to feed with greed and lust and envied things, and then in despair tried simply to deny, was all this time a hunger for you!

We are mystified and gratified that this hunger that seeds our sin is hunger for you who takes our sin away!

What a wonder! What a way to run a world! Accept, we pray, our baffled thanks and our befuddled praise.

Labor Day

How odd, dear God, that we should name one day Labor when for us every day is a labor day. And yet, not odd, because it is our everyday work that baffles us and lifts us up and beats us down—a stubborn mystery that yields its secret only grudgingly, if at all.

Our teacher in Ecclesiastes asks, "What profit does one who works get from all his labor?" and answers, "That a man should eat and drink and enjoy himself in return for all his labors—that, too, is a gift from God."

Well, we seek your gift, O God, in the nooks and crannies of our workplaces and times—your light in our darkness, your shoulder under our burden, your path among the brush and boulders strewn in our path, your self among our colleagues, our bosses, our employees, and among the beggars at our door, the homeless walking our streets, the old ones and sick ones in our homes and hospitals and nursing homes, the outlaws defeated by the mystery of our everyday— and we are confounded. And, though your gift is given every day, we cannot receive it.

Give us the gift of your everyday presence, we pray, and give us the wisdom to perceive it and the courage to receive it.

The Season of In Between

Now is the season of in-between, dear God, not quite Fall, no longer really Summer. Green is still queen, long may she reign. Red and yellow and purple and even creeping brown are still her courtiers, but the rain is cold, and revolution is in the air.

School isn't serious yet, and it keeps a sense of Summer and play. Our work is still sun-bleached and sun-tanned but now begins to fade. Now we live in Summer's wake, Irish it is in its intoxication, but our grief will soon be drenched and drowned in color.

Thanks be to you, O God, for Summer and its fullness and fatness and its fruit! Praise to you, O God, for Fall. So glorious are the living and the dying and the grieving that we don't yet feel the need for Spring and hope and resurrection.

Not So Fast!

Dear God, this time of creeping red in the trees is like the day we saw the first gray in the hair of our loved one and beside the eyes the first crow's foot lines, enhancing the beauty we always knew and loved, heralding the emergence of a beauty we never suspected but always wanted. But speaking also of aging and dying, so that we say "Yes!" and "Thanks!" and "Not so fast, not yet," and "No!" all in the same breath.

Your passing seasons parade before our hearts all the seasons of our lives and give us such pleasure and such pain that we don't know whether, if we should open our mouths, we would sing praises or howl complaints for the beauty of it all—and for the sadness. One day, the seasons say you give with one hand and take with the other, and then the year turns around again to say in Spring, "You take with one hand and give with the other," and the year sings your praise in every season. But how can we, whose lives seem to be only one round of seasons with a beginning, a middle, and an end, sing praise? And how, when each season of our lives unfolds such beauty and such promise, can we not?

So here we are, good God, caught between praise and lament, and we would stay here always seeking to freeze time, except that you yourself put on the seasons of our living and our dying and, bearing both, bear us also into everlasting life. And because of that, we do give you thanks and praise, unmixed!

The Green Gives Way to Flame

The green that was wonder in Springtime but now is work-a-day gives way to flame. The weather prophets say the flame won't burn so bright this year—too dry. Last year the weather prophets said the flame wouldn't burn so bright—too wet.

Dear God, shall we not give thanks and praise that, in this all-knowing age, no one really knows the secret of the blaze that begins to burn on our hillsides and in our hearts? The burning in our hearts bears and tells the secret. Year by year, our hearts and hillsides hold their hands high and cry, "Surprise!" And year by year, we surprise ourselves again with our surprise, and we wonder why the secret of the living of things speaks itself most clearly and eloquently in the dying of things.

And why, once learning it again a hundred times, we forget, and you have to die a hundred times a day, and you do die a hundred times a day, so we might know for sure that the blazing and the burning is the breaking forth of your yearning loving, which makes and holds us all.

Leftover summer squash lounges in our gardens.

Leftover Summer Squash

O God, leftover summer squash lounges in our gardens, admiring their own cleverness at having eluded the harvest, complimenting each other's deepening shade of yellow, smug at how the earth now accommodates their shape and weight, and fending off panic as the earth which once nurtured them and cradled them now softens them, seeking their seed.

Like us, they resort to eastern philosophy to find comfort in the idea of reincarnation, until their reverie is shattered by the thought of returning as a mere gourd and then is resumed in the contemplation of achieving pumpkin-hood.

We share much with the squash, dear God—the smugness, the illusory comfort, and the panic, our version of the fear of gourditude and the fantasy of sublime pumpkin-hood. But we are also different, because we see our seed becoming fruit right before our eyes, and we realize that all that our fruit might be is not written in the seed.

And so, year by year we invent Sunday School, and though we know you love and treasure even lowly gourds, we pray that you would be with us here and now, as the ground for our striving to produce pumpkins in Jesus's name.

Your knowing our need is the seeding of our struggle.

We Struggle to Name our Need

We struggle to name our need, dear God, and know that before we ever name it, you know it, but we know also that only in our struggle to name it are you born to respond, and yet we know that your knowing of our need is the seeding of our struggle.

There is a little child in us crying out our need in the night. But we have had parenting enough. Our need is more adult. The child in us cries of powerlessness and power. We seek to fill out our littleness with fantasies of our vastness, and you are born in us.

But then we get lost in your vastness and retreat to our littleness to find ourselves once more and get lost in littleness again.

We seek an end to this swinging and a more stable place where you are you and we are we and our hands might meet and clasp. If you won't let us walk on water, teach us at least at last to swim.

O God, we cast ourselves at once too great and too small. Come to us we pray as the true measuring of our strength, the true shaping of our selves, and join our strength with yours in shaping the world you love so much for justice, for peace, and for joy.

You burn with the blazing of each leaf.

May We Speak Plainly?

You Father and Mother a universe and everything that's in it. But may we speak plainly even so and ask you some questions?

Do you hover grandly over New England, taking mild pleasure in the colorscape that paints itself here year after year, feeling pride that you're the one who began it all? Or do you burn with the blazing of each leaf and mourn the falling of each one and our mourning of each fallen one?

Do you turn the fathering and mothering of everything that's here over to us who've been here such a little while, and retire to Grand Fatherhood and Grand Motherhood to coo and kibitz and rumble and mumble how you would have done it if you were still doing it? Or do you cry out with the pain of each bringing to birth, laugh with the joy of the presence of each new thing, and cry out with the pain of each passing and our excruciating pain at each passing?

Do you throw children at us like knuckleballs and stand at a distance to laugh and laugh at the antics of us catchers as we try to figure out where they're coming from and where they're going to? Or are you in the catching, too? We just wanted to know.

But of course, month by month, year after year, we taste the broken body and spilled blood of your living and dying of your creation, and we are moved beyond belief to a wild and crazy thanksgiving.

The Whole World Sits Down Together.

The whole world sits down together at your table today. The babel of tongues ceases, but your silence is broken with the bread and the wine. We give thanks for this sitting down and this eating and this silence, spoken in your broken body and your spilled blood.

It is also our own brokenness that we eat and drink today, O God, and our own breaking, our own spilled lives, and the lives we have spilled out of hate and fear and power lust.

Praying to be forgiven and to be made whole again, we and the broken world sit at your table.

Shameful How the Hills Resemble
More and More a Dancehall

Only the willow seems to keep a sense of decency, dear God, and now even she shows a fringe of yellow underskirt. Shameful how the hills resemble more and more a dancehall—painted women, flushed cheeks!

Oaks older than our grandmothers shed their stately green only slightly more slowly than the hot-blooded maples who, even in green, exude an air of voluptuousness. Those red-veined leaves are a sure sign! The more muted oranges and purples of the oaks and the mauve of the ash trees would, by themselves, be quite dignified and restful, but the shameless red maples incite to riot.

We wouldn't make so bold as to complain, were it not for the effect on the young and the weak. Why, we know certain saplings that can't wait for August to pass in order to start the scarlet dance—and some trees old enough to know better! (But we suspect a problem in the roots).

Even then we would keep silent if we didn't begin to suspect your hand in it. When we ourselves are weakened by the display, we find ourselves suspecting praise in it— unseemly happiness at just having been alive another year, joy in the rhythms of sleeping and waking and leafing out and shading and seeding and falling and sleeping.

Would we seem narcissistic if we said we suspected the trees and you had us in mind all along, trying to lure us out of our sadness into praising, to seduce us into your happiness, to ensnare us in your joy?

We ask forgiveness for such thoughts and such suspicion, and for our feet that begin to move toward dancing, and for our hearts that begin to swell, and for our mouths that begin, painfully, to make the shapes and sounds of praise.

What's Going On?

What's really going on between you and us, dear God? We feel so often like we're caught up in a play, and we don't know the plot or how it will end or how it began or who the author is, and we haven't learned our part.

And yet, no matter what we say and no matter how we improvise, we feel like we're in the play and can't get out because of how you constantly and faithfully improvise on our improvisations.

There was a time when we thought we were about to find it all out. Actually, there have been a lot of times. We heard you'd climbed a hill to tell your truth, and we came to find out what it was.

First, you fingered all that is poor and meek and pure and yearning and persecuted in us and called it blessed, and said the kingdom was ours and we were light and salt, and we liked that a lot.

But then you looked into our hearts and not just our deeds and found the lust and greed and hate we often harbor there, and said we must be perfect as you are perfect, and we felt caught and lost.

And when we set ourselves to save ourselves with our perfections, you showed us all the sins reserved for perfect people: perfection parading itself for the purposes of pride, acts of charity designed to impress everyone and you, precious public prayers crafted to dazzle all our friends and a god who must be deaf or doesn't care.

You show us all this and convict us of all this and then you say, "Be not anxious." How can we not be anxious? What's really going on here? If it's a morality play you've written us into, then we're lost—simple as that. Even you can't save us even though it's you who made us.

But, what if it's a love story start to finish? What if that's what we all play out but haven't seen? What if this kingdom you talk about is fed and formed and framed by love?

And what if it's not some coming, dazzling, terrifying thing but just the way things always really are between you and us—a promise always made and always kept, and we've always lived as if it weren't so, as if something else was true.

If this is what's true, then we don't quite understand our sinning or our striving to be good. Your love is very disorienting! But it's a far better thing to be lost in love than to be just lost, and we give you thanks and praise for that!

The firebush blazes away on our doorstep.

The Autumn of our Lives

The Autumn of our lives comes too fast, O God. Only yesterday was mid-Summer and an afternoon of creeping red, and when we lifted our eyes to look again, the pageant had nearly passed us by.

Then, here was this sudden nakedness fringed with gold and russet memories of what must have been. "You rained too much!" we say. "We couldn't see the mountains for days on end!" Just so do we cast the blame on you for our unlived lives, while the firebush blazes away on our doorstep.

We cry, "We can't see far enough!" You say, "Look nearby." We cry, "You don't shed enough light!" You say, "Your eye is the light of your body." We can't win this war with you that we can't lose: Love all and never a match point.

In all seasons you are so near to us that we can't see you. And in all seasons we clasp our blindness to ourselves and cry complaints.

Forgive our willful blindness, and burn so brightly on our doorstep that even we might see.

Reformation Sunday

Faith sometimes seems to be such work, dear God, that sometimes we wonder why it's worth it. There is so much in us that just wants to lay our head on your breast and finger the softness of your arm just above the elbow where once hard muscle turns tender with age, O dear Grandmother God. And we know that there is that softness and tenderness in you and the desire to hold us to your breast.

We've tasted it when we were very little and needed it very much.

But we also remember how, after a little while, our muscles began to tense and twitch and squirm us, aching for the playing that was the learning and the practicing for the work we would have to do. And we jumped down and ran off, knowing without thinking that tenderness would always be there when we needed it.

Just now it comes to us that there came a day when we climbed down and ran off to play and never went back to crawl into your lap again. There was no thought in it. We didn't exactly decide to do it, but we didn't fall either, and we weren't pushed except by our own teasing muscles. It just seemed right.

It didn't occur to us at that time that you also had other work to do with us and that the work that we went off to play at was work you had for us to do with you. And that's just it, dear God, the center of our complaint: we have the work in plenty and do it, by and large. It's you we miss. How, when you're no longer lap and breast for us are you for and with us, now?

It's not enough that you should stand back and come to judge only when our work is done and there is no more time. Our faith needs your presence now so it will not be just one more job of work.

Forgive us. We pray as if it were you and not ourselves who is somehow absent from our work. We pray as if you don't already share the burden of our flesh and soul, bear our yoke of work with us, our pain of loss, our fear of loneliness and death, our death, and so sharing, give us life and life all new.

Open our ears to hear in our own cries for your presence in our life and work your call for our presence.

Season us with yourself.

Salt

"You are the salt of the earth," you say. You say salt, but when gods come near, we expect whole worlds to be remade. But you say salt.

We would slay dragons for you, search and destroy your enemies, and you say salt. We would proclaim kingdoms and empires and democracies in your name, and you say salt. We want to be the main dish, and you say salt.

Oh, dear God, we want much more than you offer—and much less. We want to be more than you demand and much less. We can't believe that loving our neighbors and our enemies is enough, and yet we're overwhelmed by the burden of it.

What is this salt that you say and you are? The painful drawing and healing of the world's wounds? The preservation of all that sustains us? The leaping of taste to our tongues and pleasure to our bodies and feeling to our hearts and ideas to our minds and deeds to our hands and feet?

And that one word, said as if in jest, shows us who we are and just how we are loved.

Come among us, season us with yourself, then shake us out to season the world you love so much.

Dazzled With This Fall

You have dazzled us continually with this Fall, Dear God. How is it that we also grieve and wish for some other season not followed by Winter when we've been surrounded by such a rising crescendo of color?

Our imaginations leap to grasp and match the clarity of this air and light, and our bodies try to leap for the vigor promised and demanded by the cold that we have already tasted. And yet, how is it that we can also give you praise for the prospect of coming nakedness, and these premonitions of dying?

We truly don't know whether, in Fall, we fall down or fall up, and so we find ourselves singing dirges of praise and joyful songs of sorrow. We are Eve, and we are Adam, snatching up this shining apple of a season. Shall we chew? Shall we swallow and dare the dying?

Can we bear the knowing of the nakedness we soon will share with the trees?

The falling of this Fall renews our knowing that we have chewed and we have swallowed, and we have covered ourselves with fig leaves of innocence in order not to know what we know about the secrets of living and falling and dying.

Dear God, we couldn't bear the knowing of what we know, if we didn't also know that you yourself have eaten the apple and borne the nakedness and dared the dying, and that, by doing so, you have clothed us in courage for the living of these dazzling, dying, days.

We've entered the quiet time.

The Quiet Time

The year that once budded and blossomed and then burgeoned and then blazed away lies fallow before us and around us and in us. We've entered the quiet time, the waiting. If we could, we'd leap out of this early November time when nothing happens—some of us into the lively dead of Winter and Christmas, some of us into far and plastic Florida—anywhere, anytime but now and this waiting.

But the month still has business with us and we with it. And the waiting that now seems like merely waiting will soon show itself to be a gathering. Even this meal we make of you today is a gathering of grace, a stashing of grace against the storm that will come but hasn't yet.

Up to now, the year so busy with itself, matching our busyness and carrying us along, has supported us in our headlong lives. But now it has simply stopped, leaving us up in the air with our feet still moving—inviting us to stop, too.

But stop to what? Once, when we were all farmers and if we had done our work well, our busyness would have stopped with the year's, and we would have known without asking. But now our busyness won't let us stop. Our feet must move, even in the air, and this waiting time means pain for us who can only take and make and consume and spend but can never wait and gather and save.

So stop us, God. Sit us down. Maybe slap us upside of the head.

Turn our eyes and hearts and hands to gather the fruits and wounds of the busyness of this year and shape us, fruits and wounds and all, towards Thanksgiving.

Because if we can't stop and wait and gather and give you thanks, there won't be any room in us for you stirring and birthing brand new among us, breaking the busy circling of our lives' years and giving them sense and song.

Shining saints hover over our heads.

Halloween and All Saints Day

This early dawning, dark grey November day marks a boundary for us, O God. Calendars to the contrary, on this day, light and dark divide and merge. Shining saints hover over our heads. Shining saints' dark shadows—demons, hobgoblins, and things that go bump in the night—haunt and loom and skitter, scaring us to death and laughter.

Knowing and not knowing how good attracts evil, how light beckons the darkness, we ourselves have long since given up shining sainthood, as we prefer instead a middle way that seeks to buy a moderation of evil with a moderation of our good, with soft light softening the shadows.

We honestly don't know whether to brag about it or confess it.

We are loath to pray that you would cast your light upon us, for fear of the darkness we might see ourselves to be. And yet, the grey overcomes us. Numbs us.

So it is with fear and trembling that we pray that you would make us brave enough to see the light, to see the dark, to see the light. And that in your light the dark visages that haunt this day might prove to be just masks that hide the laughing faces of our children and of your child, Jesus Christ, who holds both the darkness and the light.

Right On The Tips Of Our Tongues

Although we speak your name readily, O God, to say and do your meaning and your desiring eludes us, overwhelms us.

We have you right on the tips of our tongues and open and shut our mouths around you, and you dance away, laughing tears. We step gracelessly to dance away after you, and the ground opens up beneath our feet, and we cry out for fear of falling—and fall! But we find ourselves flying instead with grace borrowed from a bird, and laughing tears, we land.

We think you're leading us on, and we want to follow! And so we pray for wings and for your breath to bear us up.

Weave the things that make for peace.

Veterans Day

You are the only veteran of all the wars that ever were, dearest God. How terrible that must be for you who aren't armored as we are, who can't divide enemies from loved ones as we can, who can't transform persons into numbers as we can, who can't separate causes from their effects, ends from means as we can and do, who exults in the flight of each single sparrow and suffers the falling of every fallen one.

How awful it must be for you in these present wars, your Muslims killing your Christians and your Jews, your Christians and your Jews killing your Muslims, your Christians killing your Christians, your Jews killing your Jews, your Muslims killing your Muslims—and all in your name, again!

How can you bear the hatred in the hearts of some of those who carry you to war with them or the emptiness and the terror and the cruelty of those who do but do not know they do?

How do you, who have been through this over and over again since the beginning of time, remain faithful to the love in which you create and hold and save the world—the love which must mean such pain for you, the love at work right now to weave the things that make for peace around the things that make for war?

And, most mysterious of all, how can you also accompany us when we must go to war? How do you, as we know you do, buttress our courage, sustain us in our best humanity? How do you guard us against the human capacity for evil which we share? How do you continue to hold us in the forgiving and healing love which we know you hold our enemies, too, when we succumb to the evil? How do you work healing in us, in our enemies, and in all our families when the strife is over?

We know that this is how you are God for us, and we give you thanks and praise for it. And we thank you for the honor and courage of those who've gone to war, for your care for their families while they've been gone, and for their safe return. We pray that you would hold the bodies and souls and families of those who have not returned in your everlasting arms.

How, we pray, may we who have been through so many wars keep faithful to your love, help to bear your pain, contribute to the weaving of the things that make for peace, the things that make for healing, the things that make for justice, and the things that make for a world with no more wars?

Help us, dear God, to have the courage to drop the armors that protect us from your pain and make wars possible, and to risk bearing only the armor that you bear: faithfulness, hopefulness, and love.

November Nodded Agreeably

November nodded agreeably, dear God, as she slipped into a seat next to us and ordered up an Indian pudding in honor of this spoonful-of-sugar Indian Summer, seeming endless, that set us dozing in the sun.

Eternity should be like this, O God, only greener. But now November, having given us dessert first, will order up turkey and all the fixings that will rudely awaken us to Thanksgiving Day. It's not that we don't want to give thanks, dear One. We do, in a heads-up, bet-hedging pause between scurrying around and squirreling away against the coming cold.

And it is this that makes us pray: not your lush green growing and giving and embracing, but the nervous narrowness of our ability to receive and to give you thanks.

There is shame in us, because we not only have to pray for what you already give us in such abundance but also for the courage to receive it and for the creation of new hearts in us that can sing thanksgivings that can match your giving.

We do thank you, dear God, and pray that you would accept and heal our wounded attempts to give you this thanks.

Parade before us again our poor and the poor of the world.

Dry Bones

You say to these bones, "Rise!" and our voices rage resounding, "Nos!" These bones smell! They hurt! They age! They die! We think you must mean our wispy spirits. But you say to these bones, "Rise!"

How can it be that you so love this weighty beast that stops our soaring, this snoring, sweating, seat of sin? Why do you always turn up loving what we would hate?

When we want to wish the world away with flood and fire, you seem to want to love the world so much you'd give your son, your self, to save it, and cause this flesh and bone we hate to rise again!

Dear God, we can't conceive, we can't believe, and, most of all, we can't love the world that you love. And yet, we pray that your love would once more heal our self hate and send us out to love with you the world you love so much.

Thanksgiving

We, your fatted calf of a nation, gather to give you thanks for ourselves, O God, and find Thanksgiving coming hard, because we don't know what it is we're being fatted and fitted for.

Having seen our capacity for evil, we despair of ever doing good at all. Having tasted the limits of our ability to work our will among the nations, we begin to fear ourselves powerless. And in this state of self despite, we are more of a danger and in more danger than in the days of our naïve strength.

So, parade before our eyes, we pray, our mountains and hills and rocks and even our rills, our fruited plains and mighty factories and wondrous inventions, our foremothers and forefathers and freedoms and vast possibilities, so we might see again what is good and strong in us.

And, having feasted us on our true fattedness and forged Thanksgiving in our hearts and on our tongues, then, parade before us again our poor and the poor of the world, our oppressed and our oppressing, the distorting of our goodness and the misuses of our strengths—not as some final Judgment that only relieves us of our responsibility but as the final field and truing ground of our goodness and our strength, what we have through all these centuries been being fatted and fitted for.

Thanks be to God.

We feel seed stirring.

The Season of Your Coming Among Us

Now the season of your coming among us descends upon us, O God.

We are fat with the remains of your other arrivals.

We have filled ourselves with blessings and emptied ourselves of all thanksgiving.

We want to rest and sleep now, like bears, except the season of your coming among us descends upon us, and we must begin to listen to the children for whom your coming among us is brand new so that we might be prepared for your coming among us which is always new.

We may claim that we are exhausted soil, that we lie fallow, draped in brown that was once lush and green.

But we feel seed stirring.

Plow up the frozen ground that we are.

Fertilize us!

So we, like Mary of old, might bring you forth.

Acknowledgments
by Reverend Allen M. Comstock

I want to acknowledge the presence of Arnold Kenseth hovering over my shoulder—even after he died—as, over the years, I wrote the prayers in *Seasonings.* Arnold wrote *Sabbaths, Sacraments, and Seasons,* a book of canticles and prayers I used for worship in churches I served. Professor of American studies at Amherst College, professor of modern poetry at the University of Massachusetts, Amherst; curator of the Woodberry Poetry Room at Harvard University, Cambridge, Massachustts; pastor of South Congregational Church in Amherst, Massachusetts, himself a poet and one of my mentors, Arnold Kenseth was known jokingly among us as the oldest living seventeenth-century poet.

Because poetic rhyms and rhythms emerged sometimes in my prayers, I had begun to think maybe I myself was a poet. One day, I proudly showed some of my prayers to Arnold. After taking the time to read them carefully, he turned to me and said, "As a poet, you're a pretty good pray-er." It took me a while to realize that he'd taken the great burden off my shoulders of trying to be a good poet and off my prayers of trying to make them good poems.

I hope I have managed to be a good pray-er of the prayers found in *Seasonings.*

I also want to acknowledge the patience, hard work, and creative response of Marcia Gagliardi of Haley's Publishing; of the copy editor, Eveline MacDougall; and of the proofreader, Debra Ellis.

And special thanks to my wife and life companion Linda Piper Comstock for support and, as she snapped the author photo on the next page, for making me smile.

photo by Linda Comstock

Allen M. Comstock

About the Author

Allen M. Comstock grew up in Huron, Ohio and graduated
from the College of Wooster in 1964. He earned his master of
divinity degree in 1968 and a master of arts in philosophical
theology in 1972 at the Hartford Seminary, Hartford,
Connecticut. He has been a pastor for fifty years, mostly
in the hill-towns of western New England. *Seasonings*
collects pastoral prayers written for worship services over
that time. He and his wife, Linda, live in Shelburne Falls,
Massachusetts.

About the Illustrator

Cara B. Hochhalter grew up in Michigan and graduated from the University of Michigan. Her careers have involved education, art, theology, and ministry. As an artist, she exhibited watercolors of endangered wildflowers in northern Michigan and Washington state.

After eight years as a United Church of Christ Christian Educator in Charlevoix, Michigan, she attended United Theological Seminary of the Twin Cities, New Brighton, Minnesota, to study art and theology. She received a master of divinity degree in 2008. While studying, she created block prints and watercolors interpreting scripture as well as issues of social justice.

In 2008, she became pastor for the Charlemont Federated Church in Massachusetts. She retired in 2018 to focus on making her art. Cara lives in Hyde Park, New York, with her husband, Jeffrey.

Colophon

Text for *Seasonings* is set in Bookman Old Style, a serifed font designed for Monotype in 2001 by Ong Chong Wah. The origins of Bookman Old Style lie in the typeface called Oldstyle Antique, designed by A. C. Phemister circa 1858 for the Miller and Richard Foundry in Edinburgh, Scotland.

Many American foundries made versions of the type, which eventually became known as Bookman. The Bookman Old Style font family is a legible and robust text face.

Titles and captions for *Seasonings* are set in Century Gothic, a digital sans serif typeface in the geometric style, released by Monotype Imaging in 1991. Century Gothic is a redrawn version of Monotype's own Twentieth Century, a copy of Bauer's Futura, to match the widths of ITC Avant Garde Gothic. It is an exclusively digital typeface that has never been manufactured as metal type.